The B Metaphysics and Neuroscience: Sam Harris vs. Thomistic Psychology

R. L. Miller Jr.

Published in the United States by the Blue Ridge Mountains
Philosophy Group.

**Blue Ridge Mountains
Philosophy Group**℠

ISBN-13: 9781796941371

DEDICATION

This book is dedicated to my loved ones, my family, and to all interested in seeking the truth in the field of neuroscience and it's intersection with the fields of philosophy, theology, psychology, and beyond. It is particularly dedicated to whosoever may benefit from seeking the truth from all the sciences and how they pertain to the mind, especially through the lens of philosophy.

PREFACE

It is the purpose of this book to be useful in contending for reality. It is for anyone wondering their stance on faith and neuroscience. It is for those seeking a response to Sam Harris' claims all too often neglected in religious and academic spheres.

This book will be an especially helpful *primer* to those in clinical, pastoral, counseling, and other professional settings where mindfulness is an accepted therapy. It is prominently used in religious counseling such as within Christian counseling and psychology integration.

Though this is a philosophical book, it is friendly for spiritual seekers, religious skeptics, and Christians who value deep thinking, yet seek to balance the tension of brevity and understandable terms, with enough depth to at least bring to surface and clarify the level of attacks upon religion in general, and in particular upon the theistic and the Christian intellect from a specific leading popular atheistic worldview under the specific pretense of neuroscience. It is my goal to introduce the neglected field of classical philosophy (Ancient Greek and Medieval) to bear upon this contemporary popular form of neuroscience.

ACKNOWLEDGMENTS

I would like to acknowledge my wife and children who welcome the participation in the engaging discussions about this topic. I would like to thank my wife again for helping proof read the final manuscript.

My first official experience with militant atheism was in my first philosophy of religion course in my freshman year of public college in Massachusetts. The goals of this course were to disprove Christianity, disprove Jesus' resurrection, and disprove God's existence.

It was after returning from the Post 9/11 war in Iraq, and witnessing the devastation of Hurricane Katrina, that I came to deeply appreciate the field of psychology through the writings of contemporary philosophers and psychologists. Having worked in the medical, healthcare, counseling, and consulting fields, I developed a deeper interest, and also came to appreciate the increasing role neuroscience is playing in so many areas of life in this era.

It was a prominent philosopher that confirmed my suspicion that one should seek a foundation in good philosophy and theology while embarking to uncover the war waged on the Christian and Theistic worldviews from scholars and clinicians from the "science" realm. Neuroscience is a friend to the arts and sciences, but all to often bad philosophy creeps into every good field of study. It can often be difficult to separate the bad philosophy from the assertions made by those who are considered as authorities in those fields.

I would like to also acknowledge my appreciation for my academic instructors in the various studies I have undertaken, who have helped me reshape my understanding of good philosophy and psychology.

"Never Forget" was the slogan Americans chanted shortly after the rubble was whisked away and the dust began to settle after that tragic September 11, 2001 day. This image is still to this day posted on social media for memorial. Disaster relief workers and psychological first aid responders are trained to understand phases of recovery. The heroic phase happens immediately after the event, when emergency crews show up on the scene. The honeymoon phase is when the media, government, and crisis responders arrive following a critical incident. Then comes the disillusionment phase, when volunteers leave, anniversaries trigger grief, and responders and media go back to their normal

routine. The last phase of reconstruction is when things get rebuilt. After September 11th, America vowed to "Never Forget." It seemed that most Americans were unified in concluding the attack was morally wrong. The media blasted the famous picture of the steel columns that made the image of a cross as dust and debris lay all around it. Many people of faith awakened, and united, with new purpose, and many went off to war to fight for what they believed was moral and just: suppressing terrorism, and tyranny, desiring to free many from the oppression of the Islamic terror.

The Global War on Terrorism went on with troops still overseas. America was standing united. Still, many were searching for answers. In 2004, neuroscientist Sam Harris published *The End of Faith: Religion, Terror, and the Future of Reason.*[1]

---

[1] Sam Harris, *The End of Faith: Religion, Terror, and the Future of Reason* (New York: W.W. Norton & Company), 2004.

As many in our nation were rallying for faith, Sam
Harris was rallying against it. So, how does 9/11 &
The End of Faith relate to the philosophy of mind?
Because Harris' hostility towards the Christian faith
is really an underlying philosophy of mind under the
guise of his research interests in neuroscience. As
will be seen, Harris' claims about neuroscience are
essentially claims within philosophy of religion, and
in particular, metaphysical. And what this author
wants to explore is just what overall system of
philosophy is underlying Harris' philosophy of
mind, his philosophy of nature, and ontological
belief system.

Regarding the nature of belief, in 2004,
Harris writes,

> The human brain is a prolific generator of
> beliefs about the world. In fact, the very
> humanness of any brain consists largely in
> its capacity to evaluate new statements of

propositional truth in light of numerous others that it already accepts.

Harris asserts that human beliefs come from the brain. That includes but is not limited to beliefs about faith, beliefs about God, beliefs about morals & ethics, beliefs about law, beliefs about economics, beliefs about science, and beliefs about human nature. All of these types belief are produced by the brain in Harris' view.

Harris asks, "What neural events underlie this process? What must a brain do in order to believe that a given statement is *true* or *false*? We currently have no idea."[2] These questions help Harris' philosophical presuppositions become more clear. As a neuroscientist, Harris may not be aware of his philosophical underpinnings, and so it would put his views at a disadvantage to be exploited upon a philosophical analysis. However, the focus of this

2Harris, *The End of Faith, 51.*

4

manuscript is not to analyze Sam Harris' awareness to his philosophical beliefs, but to expose them as significant principles supporting his premises and conclusions about consciousness and the mind.

When he asks, "What neural events cause beliefs?" this is a loaded question, presupposing and implying neural events cause beliefs. In asking "what must a brain do to believe?" implies (1) that physical brains believe, (2) immaterial does not exist, and (3) some chronological order of causality that brain events come prior to belief. Harris seems to confuse descriptive with prescriptive when referring to brain events. Does cognitive mapping explain deterministic physical causal powers, or rather express the effects of something more transcendent, such as mental events or psychological states? Why is it that in Harris' system, brain events couldn't occur simultaneously with, or after the intellectual act of belief? And why is all of this important?

Because as will be discussed, Harris' philosophy of mind, is wrapped up in his entire worldview, which contains his philosophy of nature, and his ontological belief system, and this leads him to make determinations that have profound ethical, practical, and spiritual consequences for not only him, but also for his readers. As we will see, Panpsychism is a critical subject in philosophy of religion that should not be ignored. Pansychism "literally means that everything has a mind."[3]

Like previous wars, the people of our nation grew tired of US military loss of life. With much of the mainstream media propaganda, drawing attention to isolated incidents accusing some for war crimes, disillusionment of many of the American people began to set in. It was a perfect opportunity for leaders to step up to guide the nation in morality,

[3]Panpsychism," in Standford Ecyclopedia of Philosophy. May 23, 2001. Rev. July 18, 2017. http://plato.stanford.edu/entries/panpsychism/ [Last Accessed February 28, 2019].

and remind its people of its moral heritage. In steps
Harris published another book, *Letter to a Christian
Nation,* in which he displayed his resentments
towards Christianity in particular, and metaphysics
in general stating,

> Isn't it time we admitted that this arithmetic
> of souls does not make any sense? The naïve
> idea of souls in a Petri dish is intellectually
> indefensible. It is also morally indefensible,
> given that it now stands in the way of some
> of the most promising research in the history
> of medicine. Your beliefs about the human
> soul are, at this very moment, prolonging the
> scarcely endurable misery of tens of millions
> of human beings.
> You believe that life starts at the moment of
> conception. You believe that there are souls
> in each of these blastocysts and the interests
> of one soul – the soul of a little girl with
> burns over 75 percent of her body, say –

cannot trump the interests of another soul, even if that soul happens to live inside a Petri dish. Given the accommodations we have made to faith-based irrationality in our public discourse, it is often suggested, even by advocates of stem cell research, that your position on this matter has some degree of moral legitimacy. It does not. Your resistance to embryonic stem cell research is uninformed . . . We should throw immense resources into stem-cell research, and we should do so immediately. Because of what Christians like yourself believe about souls, we are not doing this. . .

The moral truth here is obvious: anyone who feels that the interests of a blastocyst just might supersede the interests of a child with

a spinal cord injury has had his moral sense
blinded by religious metaphysics.4

It was nearly a decade after the September
11th attacks on the World Trade Center, the
Pentagon, and airplanes, declared by radical Muslim
extremists, that Harris penned a book called *The
Moral Landscape: How Science Can Determine
Human Values*.5 These books are not a
philosophical debate limited to academic circles.
You will find these books at the focal points of
Barnes and Noble stores in the spirituality and
science sections.

In *Moral Landscape,* Harris wasted no time
explaining his philosophy of mind, in terminology
that he reports to be scientific research but are

4Sam Harris, *Letter to a Christian Nation.* 2nd ed.
(New York: Vintage Books, 2008), 31-32.

5Sam Harris, *The Moral Landscape: How Science
Can Determine Human Values* (New York: Free Press, 2010).

themselves propositions "beliefs about facts and beliefs about values seem to arise from similar processes at the level of the brain."[6] Regarding the same, Harris asks, "What must we do to believe . . . What in other words must a brain do to accept such propositions as true?"[7] This is the same question that he asked in *The End of Faith.* At this point, in 2010, Harris has written his third New York Times Bestseller, and he was being more direct with his philosophy of mind. He claims,

> We are not likely to find a region of the
> human brain devoted solely to belief. The
> brain is an evolved organ, and there does not
> seem to be a process in nature that allows for
> the creation of new structures dedicated to
> entirely novel modes of behavior or
> cognition. Consequently, the brain's higher-

[6]Harris, *The Moral Landscape*, 11.

[7]Ibid., 14.

order functions had to emerge from lower
order mechanisms.8

From (1) *The End of Faith, (2) Letter to a
Christian Nation,* and (3) *The Moral Landscape,* the
picture that is painted by Harris, is one of a mixture
of evolutionary biological naturalism. There are also
quasi elements of materialism, monism, and what
philosopher James Madden calls, *weak ontological
reduction*, having mental states emerging from the
brain.9 It is Naturalism in the fact that everything is
caused by natural physical process. It is biological
in that Harris relies on evolution and natural
selection to carry out the process. Does Harris
believe consciousness is ontologically reduced or
causally reduced, or something else? Is this a form
of physicalism? Either way, to him, the brain causes

8Harris, *The Moral Landscape*, 119.

9James D. Madden, *Mind, Matter & Nature: A
Thomistic Proposal for the Philosophy of Mind* (Washington:
The Catholic University of America Press, 2013), 174-175.

the cognitive effects. We are still left with discovering what Harris' view of consciousness is. Yet, Harris is clear about there being an underlying physical and neuronal cause.[10]

In 2014, Harris published *Waking Up: A Guide to Spirituality Without Religion*. The main thesis of the book is that religion is not necessary to live a fulfilled conscious life. Harris claims all that is needed is science, including mindfulness, which is a label of a practice discovered in the Eastern religion of Buddhism, but Harris claims it is empirical science. Mindfulness is increasing in popularity in both secular and faith-based psychological treatments, as will be discussed further.[11]

The philosophy of mind dialogue is complex in that it is (1) a very old discussion, (2) has many

[10]Madden, *Mind, Matter & Nature,* 189.

[11]See also practitioners Jon Kabat-Zinn, Jeffrey M. Schwartz, and Ellen Langer in Bibliography section.

overlapping disciplines and fields of study, (3) involves many levels of philosophical and scientific topics such as consciousness, introspection, the self, the will, the intellect, etc. Harris' viewpoint is couched in heavy metaphysical terminology, and philosophy of religion/philosophy of nature, which he mostly denies. The attempt of this book is (1) to show that Harris' assertions of neuroscience that he uses to (a) prove the nature of mind and (b) undermine Christianity is not all science, (2) that his attacks on metaphysics are self-defeating and inconsistent, and (3) to offer an alternative lens to his viewpoints through moderate realism, and Thomistic psychology.

Sam Harris is not the first contemporary neuroscientist to attempt to solve the mind/body problem by integrating science and philosophy. To appreciate the complexity of the subject, Edward Hundert in 1990 wrote *Philosophy, Psychiatry, and Neuroscience: Three Approaches to the Mind: A synthetic Analysis of the Varieties of Human Experience* to "propose a single, unified theory from these three disciplines . . . how contemporary research in psychiatry and neurobiology can be understood as a natural continuation of Hegel's nineteenth century critique of Kantian philosophy."[12] We have come a long way in scientific discovery since Aristotle's *De Anima's* treatment of soul psychology and the mind. Neuroscience is now a very popular and attractive field of academics, especially with advances in robotics, artificial intelligence, mechatronics, and cognitive science, and also making stronger demand for bio-ethicists.

Hundert wrote in 1990, "Only now has neuroscience actually begun to set constraints on

[12]Edward M. Hundert, *Philosophy, Psychiatry, and Neuroscience: Three Approaches to the Mind: A Synthetic Analysis of the Varieties of Human Experience.* (New York: Oxford University Press, 1990), back cover.

acceptable theories of mind."[13] He tells of
neuroscientists beginning to make their presence felt
in philosophy, writing,

> New journals seem to appear almost daily,
> defining separate fields of neuro-anatomy,
> neuro-physiology, neuro-endocrinology, neuro-
> chemistry, and a host of subspecialties from
> other disciplines.[14]

Hundert does not shy away from talking about
the contributions and credit of philosophy on this
matter, stating that

> Philosophy has always stimulated scientific
> discoveries, but never more urgently than with
> the current arrival of that science whose explicit

---

[13]Hundert, *Philosophy, Psychiatry, and Neuroscience*,
1-5.

[14] Ibid., 1-5.

aim is to reveal the neural basis of human
thought and behavior.[15]

Although a different philosophical approach
than Hundert, Harris' aim is similar to Hundert's;
only Harris does not seem to give much credit to the
field of philosophy in his works, as potentially
might be due. Twenty-five years ago Hundert, wrote
about the "current arrival" of neuroscience. As
Hundert attempted integrating Hegelian philosophy
with neuroscience, in the same way, Harris seeks to
not only integrate, but seemingly identify the
Buddhist philosophy (a metaphysic) of mindfulness
as the pinnacle of neuroscience, while claiming that
his theory of mind does not require faith, and that
metaphysics is no longer needed.

Hundert defended the three disciplines that
he sought to synthesize, addressing "similar
questions about the mind." He sought to "discover

[15]Hundert, *Philosophy, Psychiatry, and Neuroscience*,
6.

the different limits to the sort of answers we can expect from each one." Hundert says, "The key to a synthesis of the three is solving this limit setting problem. It is *a philosophical* problem . . . built from advances in philosophy, psychiatry, and neuroscience . . . as a contribution to philosophy."[16]

Harris does not see it as a synthesis problem, nor does he see it as a philosophical problem. Rather, he sees it as a religious problem, particularly a theistic problem, and claims that metaphysics no longer belongs in the discussion. It is clear the primacy of metaphysics within Harris' view points. Therefore, limits and parameters must be acknowledged in the field of neuroscience, since it does rely on metaphysical principles, even while claiming to be pure science.

[16]Hundert, *Philosophy, Psychiatry, and Neuroscience*, 9-10.

Harris' philosophy of mind is more developed in his most recent book on the market called *Waking Up: A Guide to Spirituality Without Religion*.17 For Harris, *Waking Up* is much more explicit of his philosophy of mind. *Waking Up* is a philosophy of mind just as much, if not far more than it is a science or spirituality book, as it claims to be. What Harris calls science seems more a pseudo-science, even (unsurprisingly to metaphysicians) more of a philosophy of being, under scientism. In *Waking Up,* Harris makes claims that the Eastern Religion, Buddhism, is an *empirically verified* and a valuable *science* of the *mind*, and that Christianity is merely "metaphysical baggage."18 Harris is guilty of the very thing that he attacks most in all his writings; relying on philosophy and religiosity for science. Harris is

17Sam Harris, *Waking Up: A Guide to Spirituality Without Religion* (New York: Simon & Schuster, 2014).

18Harris, *Waking Up*, 30.

religious in the context of being devoutly committed to a belief that is based on faith, and without any empirical support. Philosophy of mind is complex. It attempts to integrate a variety of ongoing discoveries from various disciplines and sub disciplines into a whole. It appears that often, the limits that Hundert was seeking to employ are not respected by views of those such as Harris, potentially violating scientific limits (things observable) to things unobserved.

He writes that Western contemplative insights are metaphysical ideas "inspired in ignorant and isolated peoples of the past."[19] The running theme throughout Harris' mentioned books is to target mainstream Christianity, and overgeneralize it with all theistic claims, and assert that all religious philosophy of mind is "dualistic" and "faith-based," and that only in the Eastern spiritual traditions can

[19]Harris, *Waking Up,* 32-33.

one transcend dualism.[20] Is this theory correct? What about Thomas Aquinas? Was his philosophy of mind dualistic? In *Concerning Being And Essence,* Aquinas writes that there are not two distinct realities, but rather there are different modes of being, (1) composite substances, and (2) simple substances.[21] That which is the First Cause of existence, is simple, is existence itself (act), and everything else depends on and receives existence (act and potency) from the First Efficient Cause of all other being.[22] God and man are not entirely different realities. Man participates in God's reality, analogically.[23] In accordance with Thomas Aquinas,

[20]Harris, *Waking Up,* 21.

[21]Thomas Aquinas, *Concerning Being and Essence (De Ente et Essentia)* (1953; repr., New York: D. Appleton-Century Company, 1937), 37.

[22]Ibid., 25.

[23]Norman Geisler. *Systematic Theology*, Vol. 2. (Minneapolis: Bethany House, 2003), 17-23.

human nature as composed, is hylomorphic,
consisting of form and matter. Robert Brennan,
philosophical psychologist, explains the simple
nature of the human soul. He says that it has no
parts, nor is it attached to any body part, nor is it *in*
the body.24 However Brennan explains, it is present
to every part of the body.25 Does a compound
substance entail dualism since it has two parts? Not
when one understands that the Aristotelian-
Thomistic idea of mind and body are not two
different essences, nor are they divided parts of
man. Rather, modern Thomist John Madden argues
that the soul & the body are not different
substances, but the soul is *virtually* present through

24Although not exact, an analogy to explain what it is
not like, is that of an invisible peanut inside a shell, because
the soul is throughout the body, but non-extended.

25Robert Brennan, *Thomistic Psychology: A
Philosophical Analysis of the Nature of Man.* (New York:
Macmillan Company, 1953), 311-313.

the body.[26] Present that is, through the existence of God. Human nature is act (existence) and potency (possibility to exist or not). However, God IS, and God is Pure Act itself. In Aquinas, the substance of man is composed of soul and body, form and matter. Yet, the soul is not composed of itself, it is the form of the human. Since the form is simple and not composed, it does not decompose. Yet, because it receives existence, it is reliant upon the First Cause for existence. Therefore, the correct interpretation of human nature hylomorphism is not dualistic. The formal cause of human (soul) is distinct from the material cause of human (brain/body). Human nature is soul and body united in one substance, receiving existence from one dynamic act.

Harris views human essence and existence, as one with all existence in what he calls

[26]Madden, *Mind, Matter & Nature, 275.*

"consciousness." In *Waking Up*, Harris says, "Our minds are all we have. They are all we ever had."[27] He explains that it was his experience with the drug ecstasy that enlightened his conciousness to experience love as a "state of being," rather than a feeling.[28] If Harris was not a naturalist, then one might think he is an idealist. However, Panpsychism is known to be prevalent with naturalist philosophers.[29]

Harris' first experience in contemplative solitude made him think he says, not of anything philosophically or psychologically deep, but merely a "cheeseburger and milkshake." It is precisely this "human subjectivity, and nature of experience" as evidence that nothing in his book *Waking Up* "must

[27]Harris, *Waking Up,* 2.

[28]Ibid., 3.

[29]Ibid., 189.

be accepted by faith."30 As stated before, Harris views concisousness as all there is. This is a form of ontological monism. All being, according to Harris is one, and it is mind. Should we take Harris' experiences of cheeseburger paradise, and flirtation with substance abuse as a scientific theory to base our view of reality on? His longing is for real food enjoyed through the pleasure of the senses. His expectation of something strictly spiritual or immaterial; i.e. the form or blueprint of food, as a psychological experience seems nothing more than an explanation of a deep longing for the form of cheeseburgerness or milkshakeness, but not as a mere idea of the mind only, but more so because he has experienced the satisfaction of the blueprint of the food being united with material. The only way Harris knows about cheeseburgers and milkshakes is because he has experienced them in reality where

30 Harris, *Waking Up,* 1-7.

the human senses became one with the universals of burger and milk in the mind. The only way he knows epistemologically cheeseburger and milkshake is because he and they exist in reality in the relationship of form and matter, act and potency and their reality impressed upon Harris' senses. It takes both immaterial and material, not one or the other. Reality is both, and this is a Thomistic existential metaphysics and moderate realist epistemology. But Harris as philosopher is denying this type of reality and knowledge of it. Harris' metaphysical view entails that his desire for food is either reduced to material being, and a physical process that causes all states of being, or at least in consistency with his version of Panpsychism, that his conciousness of the cheeseburger and milkshake was all there was. Yet, in line with emergentism, conciousness may emerge from the material, yet with Harris, it seems naturalistically and ontologically identical to conciousness. For Harris, there is no form in the matter. According to moderate realism, Harris would be knowing and experiencing both the universal immaterial form within the particular matter (cheeseburger and milkshake). Therefore, it is Harris' interpretation of metaphysics (monism and naturalism), his ontological presuppositions, that underly and determine what he calls scientific and spiritual observation. In spite of Harris' skeptisicm of metaphysics, he relies on metaphysics heavily. Whether he does it intentionally or not, or is just not being forthright with his knowledge is not the subject of this book.

Regarding Harris' view of conciousness, he states that there is no "I" or "self" in the brain. He argues for conciousness itself over the "feeling" of "I."[31] The theory of the self has been a long running theory in Cartesian philosophy and Jungian

[31]Harris, *Waking Up,* 10, 81.

26

psychology. It would seem that Harris objects to the self for two reasons. First, Carl Jung's focus on self-actualization was "based on unexamined philosophical and moral assumptions," says psychologist, Paul Vitz.[32] Secondly, Buddhism, which Harris embraces, denies the self (the "atman") in favor of experience itself, which eventually led to the bundle theory of the mind.[33] Harris says he is leaving behind metaphysics, and finds the practice of mindfulness to be relieving. Mindfulness being the development of Eastern religion, particularly Buddhism, which Harris prefers to call "real spirituality."[34]

[32]Paul C. Vitz, *Psychology as Religion: The Cult of Self-Worship.* 2nd ed. (Grand Rapids: Eerdmans Publishing, 1994), 4.

[33]Oxford Dictionary of Philosophy. 2nd ed. (Oxford: Oxford University Press, 2005), 49.

[34]Harris, *Waking Up,* 13-35.

According to Harris, conciousness emerges without any change in material (brain), leaving a first person experience.[35] Harris believes that he has stumped Christian metaphysicians by bringing in the split-brain theory or phenomenon, whereby the cerebral hemispheres become separated. Harris claims that evidence suggests that there are then two indpendent beliefs, and cognitive abilities in two separate parts of the brain at the same time. Harris believes that split brain does not effect concisousness, and that concisousness is all that matters, as conciousness is the "substance of our experience," which emerges from the brain, as a subjective first person experience, yet not irreducible to the brain, and without causing changes in the brain.[36]

[35]Harris, *Waking Up,* 57.

[36]Ibid., 53, 62.

When it comes to mindfulness, and conciousness, Harris is not alone. Psychiatrist, and UCLA researcher of neuroplasticity, and mental force, Jeffrey Schwartz said that Buddhist philosophy and meditation grew on him in his early years.[37] However, his focus is on the brain causing new neural pathways. He views conciousness as subjective, felt, non-materialistic, and that conciousness and intentionality can cause mental force, thereby providing new brain pathways through mindfulness meditation.[38] He posits that "mindfulness-based cognitive therapy for OCD led me to posit a new kind of studyable force. I called it directed mental force . . . What mental force does is activate a neuronal circuit."[39] Thus, it apears that

[37]Jeffrey M. Schwartz, and Sharon Begley. *The Mind & The Brain: Neuroplasticity and the Power of Mental Force.* (New York: Harper Collins, 2002), 18.

[38]Schwartz and Begley, *The Mind & The Brain*, 27.

[39]Ibid., 95.

Harris is correct in that mindfulness (cognitive concious awareness) is empircal, and impactful on the brain. However, this does not prove that cognition emerges from neurophysiology. Nor does the act of practicing mindfulness, being concious, introspection, etc. entail reducibility to or emergence from the brain. Furthermore, none of this denies the possibility of immaterial forms. The basis of mindfulness is the Eastern religion of Buddhism, along with its pantheistic monism.[40] As James Madden pointed out, this view, he calls Panpsychism, is for naturalistic philosophers, and "conciousness is among the fundamental properties of matter."[41]

When it comes to Harris' arguments against Christianity, and metaphysics, it appears that Harris is setting up logical straw men, in order to win more

[40]Vitz, *Psychology as Religion,* 1

[41]Madden. *Mind, Matter & Nature,* 188.

audience to his side. Defenders of embryo rights
would never devalue the "soul of a little girl" over
any other soul. This is an either-or fallacy, a.k.a.
false dilemma. Furthermore, the terminology of
"soul in" is loaded. That entails that there is a
dualist separation of soul and body. The idea Harris
is espousing that Christians hold is that of a dualist,
the soul is *in* the matter, yet separate, parallel.

This neglects that there is most probable
support for soul/body unity, that of hylomorphism,
which is a view that Harris never attempts to argue
against in any of his national bestsellers critiqued in
this book. He simply does not take up argument
against Aristotelian Hylomorphism, but simply
"metaphysics" in general. Furthermore, Harris is
guilty of ad-hominems such as poisoning the well.
This occurs by attacking values and claiming that
Christians are responsible for the "scarcely
endurable misery of tens of millions of human
beings." Harris is inconsistent, for if he held that

souls entailed human worth, then he would not view one human as more valuable than another. His morals are situational, consequentialist, in favor of "the end justifies the means," which is proven to be very dangerous and destructive as an overarching metaethic.42 Harris' views are dangerous to human existence. While he claims that Western Philosophy is inspired by ignorant people, he simply fails to recognize the history of philosophy, and that what he thinks is neuroscience is actually an eclecticism of various philosophers throughout the ages. Harris' view of the mind is an ancient philosophy couched in new science terms.43 Harris is ignorant of what Etienne Gilson calls, *The Unity of Philosophical*

42Dennis Hollinger. *Choosing the Good. Christian Ethics in a Complex World* (Grand Rapids: Baker, 2002), 35.

43"Panpsychism," in Standford Ecyclopedia of Philosophy. May 23, 2001. Rev. July 18, 2017. http://plato.stanford.edu/entries/panpsychism/ [Last Accessed February 28, 2019].

Experience.44 C.S. Lewis having was entrenched in the philosophy of his day, having experienced Oxford University, and having been a philosopher that learned in war time. He went on to teach formally as a lecturer, and is still educating minds today indirectly through his writings. Knowing the war of ideas is a matter of life and death, he stated in *Learning in War Time*, about the learned life saying that,

> If all the world were Christian, it might not matter if all the world were uneducated. But as it is, a cultural life will exist outside the Church whether it exists inside or not. To be ignorant and simple now-not to be able to meet the enemies on their own ground- would be to throw down our weapons, and

44Etienne Gilson, *The Unity of Philosophical Experience* (New York: Charles Scribner's Sons, 1950) https://www.iicss.iq/files/books/1q1c0ad8g.pdf [Last Accessed February 12, 2019].

to betray our uneducated brethren who have, under God, no defence but us against the intellectual attacks of the heathen.[45]

As a neuroscientist, Sam Harris has the perceived authority and respect from the scientific community, and the nature of his writings, being national bestsellers, are no doubt reaching many non-academics, especially those untrained in philosophy. Harris, while seemingly highly intelligent, is seemingly not habituated in identifying and applying false logic and philosophical presuppositions underlying scientific assumptions. Not to mention, there seems an unsurprising resurgence in Harris that is the metaphysical skepticism Gilson had noted in from the "late middle ages" to the "seventeenth century."[46]

[45]C. S. Lewis, "Learning in War time" in *The Weight of Glory*. Revised. (New York: Harper Collins, 1976) 58.

[46]Gilson, 77.

Harris cannot logically and consistently attack metaphysical viewpoints, while making metaphysically religious assertions. To deny that there is a soul, is not scientific, but rather philosophical. Science cannot observe what is unobservable by empirical data. The human essence that is composed of not only material (body & brain), but also form (soul). Especially in light of Thomism, it is the matter that is empirical, and the form that is immaterial. Hence, the human soul as form will not appear on any MRI. Brain, body, behavior and habits are observable. Studying being itself and the natures and essences of being is philosophical. Thus, Harris' works have been unable to disprove the existence of the human soul/spirit ontologically. Nor has he been able to scientifically observe the nature and essence of humanity as mere material or mere soul only. At the core, this is an example of the limitations of science, and systems and methodologies within philosophy of science, namely neuroscience.

Lastly, in discovering the truth in integrating philosophy, and the sciences, this is a reminder of the often quoted Arthur Holmes that "All truth is God's truth, wherever and however it be found."[47] In saying that, Holmes also regards that "perennial problems provide the matrix within which philosophy operates . . . underlie all other aspects of life and thought . . . The problem of permanence and change in the philosophy of nature, for instance did much to shape the Greek theory of universals."[48]

As noted previously, Philosopher James Madden argues, all philosophy of mind theories can really only fall into some form of one of three categories, (1) materialism, (2) Dualism, or (3) Aristotelian Hylomorphism. Madden says

[47]Arthur Holmes, *All Truth is God's Truth* (Grand Rapids: Eardmans, 1977), 67.

[48]Holmes, *All Truth is God's Truth*, 63.

philosophical naturalism "dominates contemporary thinking about the mind and problems it raises."[49] Madden states that scientism (scientific method is the only avenue to knowledge or justified belief), and naturalism (reality consists of nothing but a single, all embracing spatio-temporal system measured by scientific method, i.e. physics, chemistry, biology, etc.) are two ways of saying science is the measure of all things.[50]

Emergence and system features (Biological Naturalism) is a non-physical, conscience substance distinct from body, emerging from the body. All processes in the central nervous system are higher level processes. Lower level processes are in the brain. Yet, this is just another form of naturalism.[51]

[49]Madden, *Mind, Matter & Nature*, x-xi.

[50]Ibid., 3-5.

[51]Ibid., 176-180.

Madden shows that through John Haldane, thoughts cannot emerge from the physical because universals exist in the intellect and in agreement with Alvin Plantinga, neurophysiological processes cannot give account of logical reasoning.[52]

Following Madden's interpretation of Aristotelian Hylomorphism, the principle of actuality is what accounts for the coming to be in change. The virtual presence of a compound substance is the elements presented in the sense that their capacities not as individual parts but virtual parts of the new substance.[53] Humans are a soul body compound unity. The soul accounts for the organism's actuality, growth, nutrition, reproduction, and sensation of consciousness.[54] "The origin of the human soul is not empirically

[52]Madden, *Mind, Matter & Nature,* 208-214.

[53]Ibid., 241-242.

[54]Ibid., 255-256.

detectable, and that we can say of it is only what we can demonstrate philosophically."[55]

Philosopher John Haldane demonstrates the realist understanding that phenomenal consciousness is individuation (matter), and universality (no matter). At the intellectual level or information (universal) form, "there is no empirical instantiation. Abstract thought is structured by universals and universals only exist as such apart from (empirical) matter."[56] Thus, as Haldane argues immediately following, "intellectual powers are not physical." Haldane explains that there are not two substances in hylomorphism, but one single essence of physical and mental. Cognition happens when the person receives the form. Philosopher Eleonore

[55]Madden, *Mind, Matter & Nature,* 271-273.

[56]John Haldane, "A Return to Form in the Philosophy of Mind," in *Form and Matter: Themes in Contemporary Metaphysics,* ed. David S. Oderberg (Malden: Blackwell Publishing), 57-58.

Stump explains the cognitive intellect process from a moderate realist vantage point. She says, interpreting Aquinas, the senses receive the medium spiritually through an encoded blueprint. The senses go through material change, impressing on the internal material brain organ. Through phantasms, images produce conscious awareness, as the intellect processes encoded information by extracting and abstracting the individual particular, from the material, and leaving only information about universals.[57]

In 2003, Stump admitted that no one yet knows the components that allow humans to be conscious of the world around them, nor the methods for obtaining the data.[58] Mortimer Adler, in response to materialists, says that there is no point

[57]Eleonore Stump, *Aquinas: Arguments of the Philosophers* (New York: Routledge, 2003), 267-269.

[58]Stump, 276

of speaking of *mind,* if it has no meaning. For
Adler, if the mind is as observable as the brain, then
why use the word *mind;* but he says inferences can
be made about the mind, based on observable
behavior.59 While mindfulness may be useful, that
was not the subject of this book.

Philosopher and theologian Norman Geisler
summarizes Evangelical Christian Thomistic
metaphysics regarding consciousness,

> Human beings are reducible to neither pure
> matter nor to pure spirit. They have two
> dimensions: body and soul. Nevertheless,
> these two aspects from one nature composed
> of form and matter, and they are a
> form/body unity, not an identity. The soul
> survives the dissolution of the body and is
> conscious, albeit incompletely (apart from
> the body), between death and resurrection.

59Mortimer J. Adler. *Intellect: Mind Over Matter*.
(New York: Macmillan, 1990), 20-23.

In addition to being one in nature
(soul/body) and two in dimension (inner and
outer), human beings are three in direction:
They have self - consciousness, world-
consciousness, and God - consciousness.
Only one of these dimensions – world -
consciousness – is lost in the intermediate
state between death and resurrection. The
resurrection will restore the wholeness and
completeness of a human being as created
by God – in unity.
The human person embodied in flesh
possesses intellect, emotion, will, and
consciousness.[60]

Regarding Harris' Split-brain problem, what if
a person believed in Christ for salvation with one
brain hemisphere, and didn't believe in Jesus Christ
for salvation with the other brain hemisphere?

[60]Norman Geisler. *Systematic Theology,* Vol. 3
(Grand Rapids: Bethany House 2004), 78

Which psych state would the person be? The
problem is regarding unity of brain, and unity of
consciousness or mental duality.[61] Michael Rea's
Doctrine of Accidental Sameness may have some
solutions to the split-brain concern of Sam Harris.
Rea writes that "accidental sameness is not identity,
but a kind of numerical sameness . . . an event and a
material object can fully occupy the same region of
spacetime without sharing all of their parts in
common."[62]

    Something persists through change: form.
The form of man having no parts is not affected.
The form is like a castle rock; it remains untouched
as essence. Although faculties are needed to
experience the senses, the neural processes are

[61]Harris, *Waking Up,* 63.

[62]Michael C. Rea. *"*Sameness Without Identity*"* in
Form and Matter: Themes in Contemporary Metaphysics.
Edited by David S. Oderberg (Malden: Blackwell Publishers,
1999), 109.

accidental that share the substance with the spirit. Therefore, under Rea's view, the split brain is numerically the same as the individual, occupying the same spacetime, but the split-brain mental states needs not be identical with the individual. Split brain "problem," as Harris suggest, has an underlying naturalist assumption, that brain is either identical to or causing consciousness. The question addresses one's state of consciousness related at a neurobiological level. What about Alzheimer, Parkinson's, multiple personality, and schizophrenia, etc.? Brennan's notion of Aquinas' ontological ego may help in this case. He says that Aquinas prepared for "material substrate regularly undergoing change" which does not "challenge the permanency of his ontological person" because the accidental nature of man is grounded in the "ontological ego, in which it is rooted." Brennan states "personality does not change with each new

cognition and effect."63 In light of modern versions
of the cosmological argument, acknowledging the
need for differing modes of being (act and potency),
the Spirit of God, the mind of God, who is
unalterable, and unchangeable, pure act would
ground the ontological ego.64 Ontological ego then
makes sense, but only in the context of divine
essentialism, as grounded in the classical
cosmological argument.

The reason is in the fact that as Etienne
Gilson says, "the sufficient reason for the actual
existence of any finite being is never to be found in
that being itself; it always is to be found in another
one." 65 This is precisely why neuroscience cannot

63Brennan, *Thomistic Psychology*, 291-298.

64Norman Geisler, *God: A Philosophical Argument
from Being* (Matthews: Bastion Books, 2015), 10.

65Etienne Gilson, *Being and Some Philosophers.* 2nd
ed. (Toronto, Canada: Pontifical Institute of Medieval Studies,
1952), 119.

ever *disprove* the existence of God, nor the supernatural, nor the human soul.[66]

As shown above, the human soul is special, and permanent.   Brennan says, "In his body we have the principle of the soul's individuation. In his soul we have the principle of his body's speciation. Each has a function." Only when they are unified as complete substance, he says, "do we find perfection of complete person."[67]

[66]As a primer, focusing on human nature as a form/matter composite.

[67]Brennan, *Thomistic Psychology,* 296.

Bibliography

Adler, Mortimer J. *Intellect: Mind Over Matter*.
New York: Macmillan, 1990.

Aquinas, Thomas. *Concerning Being And Essence
(De Ente et Essentia).* New York: D.
Appleton-Century Company, 1937.

Bickel, Bruce, and Stan Jantz. *World Religions &
Cults 101: A Guide to Spiritual Beliefs.*
Eugene: Harvest House, 2002.

Blackburn, Simon. *The Oxford Dictionary of
Philosophy.* 2nd ed. Oxford: Oxford
University Press, 2005.

Brennan, Robert. *Thomistic Psychology: A
Philosophical Analysis of the Nature of
Man.*1937. Reprint. New York: Macmillan
Company, 1953.

Gilson, Etienne. *Being and Some Philosophers*. 1952. Reprint. Toronto, Canada: Pontifical Institute of Medieval Studies, 2016.

——. *Unity of Philosophical Experience*. New York: Charles Scribner's Sons, 1950. https://www.iicss.iq/files/books/1q1c0ad8g.pdf [Last Accessed February 12, 2019].

Geisler, Norman. *God: A Philosophical Argument from Being*. Matthews: Bastion Books, 2015.

——. *Baker Encyclopedia of Christian Apologetics*. 1999. Reprint. Grand Rapids: Baker, 2006.

——. *Systematic Theology*. Vol. 1, Minneapolis: Bethany House, 2002.

——. *Systematic Theology*. Vol. 2, Minneapolis: Bethany House, 2003.

———. *Systematic Theology.* Vol. 3, Minneapolis:
Bethany House, 2004.

Haldane, John. "A Return to Form in the Philosophy
of Mind." In *Form and Matter: Themes in
Contemporary Metaphysics,* edited by David
S. Oderberg, 40-64. Malden: Blackwell
Publishing, 1999.

Harris, Sam. *Letter to a Christian Nation.* 2nd ed.
New York: Vintage Books, 2008.

———. *The End of Faith: Religion, Terror, and the
Future of Reason.* New York: W.W. Norton
& Company, Inc., 2004.

———.*The Moral Landscape: How Science Can
Determine Human Values*. New York: Free
Press, 2010.

———. *Waking Up: A Guide to Spirituality Without Religion.* New York: Simon & Schuster, 2014.

Holmes, Arthur F. *All Truth is God's Truth.* Grand Rapids: Eardmans, 1977.

Hollinger, Dennis P. *Choosing the Good: Christian Ethics in a Complex World.* Grand Rapids: Baker, 2002.

Goff, Philip, Seager, William and Allen-Hermanson, Sean, "Panpsychism", The Stanford Encyclopedia of Philosophy (Winter 2017 Edition), Edward N. Zalta (ed.), https://plato.stanford.edu/archives/win2017/entries/panpsychism/> [Last Accessed February 28, 2019].

Hundert, Edward M. *Philosophy, Psychiatry, and Neuroscience: Three Approaches to the Mind: A Synthetic Analysis of the Varieties of Human Experience.* New York: Oxford University Press, 1990. [Last Accessed February 12, 2019].

Kabat-Zinn, Jon. *Coming to Our Senses: Healing Ourselves and the World Through Mindfulness.* New York: Hyperion, 2005.

———. *Mindfulness for Beginners: Reclaiming the Present Moment – and Your Life.* Boulder: Sounds True, 2012.

Langer, Ellen J. *Mindfulness.* 1989. Reprint. Boston: De Capo, 2014.

Lewis, C. S. "Learning in War-Time." In *The Weight of Glory.* Revised. New York: Harper Collins, 1976.

Madden, James D. *Mind, Matter & Nature: A Thomistic Proposal for the Philosophy of Mind.* Washington: Catholic University of America Press, 2013.

Oderberg, David S. *Real Essentialism.* New York: Routledge, 2007.

Schwartz, Jeffrey M., and Sharon Begley. *The Mind & the Brain: Neuroplasticity and the Power of Mental Force.* New York: Harper Collins, 2002.

Stump, Eleonore. *Aquinas: Arguments of the Philosophers*. New York: Routledge, 2003.

Sullivan, Daniel. *An Introduction to Philosophy: Perennial Principles of the Classical Realist Tradition.* 1957. Reprint. Charlotte: Tan, 2009.

Vitz, Paul C. *Psychology as Religion: The Cult of
Self-Worship.* 2nd ed. Grand Rapids:
Eerdmans Publishing, 1994.

ABOUT THE AUTHOR

R. L. Miller Jr. is an educator and licensed healthcare practitioner. He has taught graduate level leadership at the private college setting. He has been key note speaker at public and private college seminars, educating the military veterans continuum of care. He has completed study at the graduate level in a variety of subjects including but not limited to philosophy, psychology, religion, business, and organizational behavior. He holds multiple regionally accredited graduate and undergraduate degrees. He has served in the Middle East at the U.S. Armed Forces largest combat theater hospital caring for many of the devastating Post 9/11 injuries of war. In addition to medical centers, rehab hospitals, and clinics, he has managed and worked extensively with non profit organizational outreach for Post 9/11 combat veterans dealing with the invisible wounds of war.

He has completed supervised clinical internships serving military veterans in the outpatient clinic setting. He has in the past raised support for charities by running in races including marathons. He now occasionally serves his local community by volunteering including having recently coached children's sports, taught at religious institutional programs, and by coming along side those injured by crisis and trauma.

Printed in Great Britain
by Amazon